SAVED FOREVER

MAKING A BIBLICAL CASE FOR ETERNAL SECURITY

CHESTER TATMON, Th.D

Saved Forever: Making a Biblical Case for Eternal Security

Copyright © 2026 Chester Tatmon, Th.D

All rights reserved. No part of this publication may be reproduced, distributed, or transmitted in any form or by any means, including photocopying, recording or other electronic or mechanical methods, without the prior written permission of the author, except in the case of brief quotations embodied in reviews and certain other non-commercial uses permitted by copyright law.

For permission requests, contact: Purpose Publishing via email at contactus@purposepublishing.com.

For speaking engagements, interviews, bulk orders, or promotions contact the author and stay connected at chet60@gmail.com

Printed in the United States of America

Paperback ISBN 978-1-965319-68-0

Scriptures marked HCSB are taken from the HOLMAN CHRISTIAN STANDARD BIBLE (HCSB): Scripture taken from the HOLMAN CHRISTIAN STANDARD BIBLE, copyright© 1999, 2000, 2002, 2003 by Holman Bible Publishers, Nashville Tennessee.
All rights reserved.

Scriptures marked NKJV are taken from the NEW KING JAMES VERSION (NKJV): Scripture taken from the NEW KING JAMES VERSION®. Copyright© 1982 by Thomas Nelson, Inc.
Used by permission. All rights reserved.

Purpose Publishing LLC.

13194 US Highway 301 South, Suite 417

Riverview, Florida 33578

www.PurposePublishing.com

TABLE OF CONTENTS

Introduction 5

Chapter 1: The God of the Bible 7

Chapter 2: What is Biblical Salvation? 29

Chapter 3: Jesus the Christ 37

Chapter 4: The Role of the Holy Spirit 49

Chapter 5: The Apostles' View 54

Chapter 6: Past Centuries Theologians 65

Chapter 7: Contemporary Theologians 75

Conclusion 88

Synopsis 90

Bios 91

Acknowledgements And Dedications 92

Theological Influences and Resources 93

INTRODUCTION

In multiple Christian circles, it is taught that one can lose his or her salvation, but what is really meant by this assertion? Do they mean that if one is genuinely and truly born again that salvation can be lost? Or are they using the term saved in a different sense?

This is not a new question. Throughout Church history there have been different viewpoints on this subject. We would like to join the crowd and briefly explore this question primarily from a Biblical perspective.

However, this doesn't mean that we will not be examining the numerous scholars and theologians that have gone before us. In our view, they have much to contribute to this issue. Moreover, we believe that it is paramount that we begin with the very nature of God, allowing Him to reveal Himself to us from His word which He brought into existence. Then we will permit Jesus the Christ, who died that we might be saved in the first place, to teach us about eternal salvation. Furthermore, we will investigate the Holy Spirit's role in this matter. Also, the apostles will chime in as well.

Finally, we will call on some contemporary scholars to give their findings. Obviously, this is not an exhaustive treatment of this subject; it only serves as an introduction to an intriguing and necessary concept: "Are we saved forever?"

CHAPTER 1

THE GOD OF THE BIBLE

When we refer to the Bible, we mean the 66 books of the Protestant's Canon. Why do we emphasize the number of books? Because there are multiple schools of thought as to how many books belong in the Canon.

What does the term "canon" mean in a Christian context? Google gives the following definition: "Canon" refers to the authoritative collection of books in the Bible, derived from the Greek word "Kanon" meaning "rule" or "measuring stick."

The Biblical Canon includes the Old and New Testaments, which are considered to be divinely inspired and form the foundational standard for Christian belief and practice. We believe that God through His Spirit, used humans to record the original autographs, meaning that He superintended every aspect of it, therefore, they were without error.

We will look briefly at the composition of the Bible using materials from my book, *The Sword*:

Fifteen Hundred Years in the Making

From the composition of the first biblical book until the last, a period of fifteen hundred years elapsed. The Old Testament was written between 1400 and 400 B.C. The first book composed was either the book of Genesis or the book of Job. The books of the New Testament were written between A.D. 40 and A.D. 90.

Many Authors from Many Occupations

Over forty different human authors wrote the books of the Bible. These writers came from a variety of backgrounds and occupations. They included shepherds, (Hosea and Amos), fishermen (Peter and John), a tax collector (Matthew), a prime minister (Daniel), a doctor (Luke), and a military general (Joshua).

Different Continents

The books of the Bible were composed upon three different continents: Africa, Asia, and Europe. For example, the writings of Ezekiel were composed in Babylon (Asia), Moses wrote the first five books of the Bible in the Sinai desert (Africa), and the Apostle Paul wrote the letter to Philippi while in Rome (Europe).

Different Languages

The Bible was written in three different languages. The Old Testament was mostly written in Hebrew, with some parts being composed in Aramaic; the New Testament was originally written in Greek.

We believe that God preserved many reliable copies of it over the centuries and used human authors to select and compose the Jewish/ Christian Canon, which again, has only 66 books in it. We belabor this because this is where we will acquire our information about who God is and how He behaves, not from any additional books that have been added to some of the other Canons. For instance, Catholicism, has adopted into their Canon seven or more of the Apocrypha books. Books like 1&2 Maccabees, Tobit, Judith, and more.

Moreover, the Eastern Orthodox or Greek as it is often referred to, uses even more of these books in their Canon. Sources, report the following: "The Eastern Orthodox Church adheres to the first official canon of 73 books, as reaffirmed at the Council of Carthage (A.D. 419). This is the same Canon that the Roman Catholic Church affirms. In addition to the 73, Orthodox Christians also include 1 Esdras, 3 Maccabees, and the Prayer of Manasseh."

The Protestant community, for the most part, rejects these books as being authoritative. We highlight the term "authoritative" because many students see some benefit to reading and familiarizing oneself with these extra-biblical texts. However, remember, they are not to be used to build doctrine or practice.

As we delve into the nature of God, we will observe some of His attributes as they are revealed in the Bible: Holy, Sovereign, Aseity, Omnipotent, Omnipresent, Omniscient, Infinite, Immutable, Righteous, Just, Love, Good and a host of other qualities that are attributed to Him. Let's briefly look at each of these:

Holy

> Gotquestions.com illuminates us, "In the Hebrew, the words translated "holy" and "holiness" have to do with being "set apart," "separate," "different," or "dedicated." The absolute moral purity of God's character sets Him apart, making Him different from every other living creature… Holiness is His essence. God is morally and ethically perfect by nature."

Sovereign

> "A sovereign is a term with multiple meanings, but in general, it refers to a supreme leader or ruler." Gotquestions.com shares with us, "God's sovereignty is one of the most important principles in Christian theology, as well as one of its most hotly debated. Whether or not God is actually sovereign is usually not a topic of debate, all mainstream Christian sects agree that God is preeminent in power and authority. God's sovereignty is a natural consequence of omniscience, omnipotence, and omnipresence."

Aseity

"The word aseity literally means 'of oneself.' God is self-existent and necessary by His own very nature." In other words, God has the power of "Being" within Himself.

Omnipotent

It means "All Powerful" unlimited power. There is nothing and no one that can equal the power of God.

Omnipresent

It means being present everywhere; there is nowhere where God's presence is not fully and completely there.

Omniscient

It is defined as having total knowledge. There is nothing that escapes the knowledge of God. He knew us throughout eternity.

Infinite

This word means "unlimited." When applied to God, it refers to Him as being limitless. As human beings, we are finite; we are limited.

Immutable

According to the Oxford Dictionary: "unchanging over time or unable to be changed." The Bible teaches that God does not change. God is portrayed as saying, "For I am the LORD, I do not change." (Malachi 3:6a NKJV) It is very important that we remember this trait because it is relevant to one of the crucial points in our argument for eternal security.

Moreover, Sam Storms writes this about the good news of God's unchanging nature: "What all this means, very simply, is that God is dependable! Our trust in him is therefore a confident trust, for we know that he will not, indeed cannot, change."

Righteous

According to a Google search: "(of a person or conduct) morally right or justifiable; virtuous."

Just

Again, another Google search produces this definition: "based on or behaving according to what is morally right or fair."

Love

> Strong feelings of affection. The word mostly used in the Scripture for love is "Agape." According to Wikipedia: "Agape is a Greek word meaning 'the highest form of love, charity' and 'the love of God for [human beings] and of [human beings] for God.'"

Good

> "O taste and see that the Lord is good," Psalm 34:8: Just like his other attributes, God's goodness exists within his immutability and infinite nature so that he is unchangingly, always good. His mercy flows from his goodness. In his goodness to us, we see that He has purposed to be good in a special way to his people." (Ligonier.com)

We have not given an exhaustive account of the attributes of God; this would be impossible for anyone to do.

Lastly, we will explore briefly the following idea about God that is taught in the Scriptures, the "Trinity."

We are well aware of the different schools of thought on this particular doctrine. Moreover, we concede that the word trinity does not appear in the Bible. However, it is our view that, if one would study the Bible with as much objectivity and fairness as possible, he or she would draw the conclusion that the concept of the Trinity is there.

Many have fallen into a theological abyss of confusion because they couldn't reconcile with their finite minds how this could be; therefore, they rejected it altogether. They forgot that the finite cannot comprehend the Infinite in its completeness.

For example, Robert Morey, in his book, *The Trinity*, makes the following observations:

> "The Trinitarian begins with the *a priori* assumption that the triune God of Father, Son, and Holy Spirit will be incomprehensible because God is essentially incomprehensible in His nature. The Trinity is so deep a mystery that it forces us to our knees in wonder, awe, and praise. After all, any God we could fully understand and explain would be less than what we are. Such a God would not be worthy

of our worship, awe, and praise. The inescapable truth is that God will always be greater than our finite capacity to understand fully or to explain exhaustively."

Isaiah depicts God as saying, "For as heaven is higher than earth, so My ways are higher than your ways, and My thoughts than your thoughts." Isaiah 55:8,9 (HCSB)

Note, the concept of the Trinity is defined as one God that exists in three persons or one Essence that exists in three persons. This is not a contradiction; it is a mystery. Some further argue that it is a paradox, meaning that it is an apparent contradiction, but not a bona fide or actual one. The idea of the Trinity violates no logical rules.

Let's look briefly at how scholars and theologians work this out from the Bible. For example, Scripture teaches that there is only one God. Turn with me to the book of Deuteronomy, "Hear, O Israel: The LORD our God, the LORD is one!" Deuteronomy 6:4a (NKJV)

Moreover, Isaiah records, "Remember the former things of old, For I am God, and there is no other; I am God, and there is none like Me," Isaiah 46:9 (NKJV)

Furthermore, Isaiah records, "…That there is none besides Me. I am the LORD, and there is no other; …And there is no other God besides Me, A just God and a Savior; There is none besides Me." Isaiah 45:6b, 21c (NKJV)

There are many other verses that we could call on, but these will suffice for our illustration. So, we observe that the Bible is adamant about there being only one God. We must keep this in mind when studying the doctrine of the Trinity.

Now that the oneness of God has been established, we will proceed to the Threeness of Him. In the Old Testament, there are hints and glimpses of the Threeness of God. Let's observe a couple of verses that illustrate this: "Come near to Me, hear this: I have not spoken in secret from the beginning; From the time it was, I was there. And now the Lord God and His Spirit have sent Me." Isaiah 48:16 (NKJV) Note that there are three entities in this passage. The Father, the Son, (Me) and the Holy Spirit.

Moreover, another passage in Isaiah, suggests the presence of the three persons of the Trinity: "The Spirit of the Lord God is upon Me, Because the LORD has anointed Me to preach good tidings to the poor…" Isaiah 61:1b (NKJV) From our observation, the text identified, "the Spirit," the "Lord God," and "the Me," which is referencing the second person in the Trinity. For more clarity on this passage, go to the Gospel of Luke 4:18-21 (NKJV)

There are multiple verses in the New Testament that seem to support the doctrine of the Trinity.

First, let's observe the Scripture that records the baptism of Jesus: "When He had been baptized, Jesus came up immediately from the water; and behold, the heavens were opened to Him, and He saw the Spirit of God descending like a dove and alighting upon Him. And suddenly a voice came from heaven, saying, 'This is My beloved Son, in whom I am well pleased.'" Matthew 3:16,17 (NKJV)

Notice that we have all three persons represented in this passage: Jesus in the water, the Holy Spirit descending in the form of a dove, and the Father speaking from heaven. All Three persons are present here: Father, Son, and Holy Spirit.

Lastly, in this same book the 28th chapter, this is popularly known as Jesus' great commission: "Go therefore and make disciples of all the nations, baptizing them in the name of the Father and of the Son and of the Holy Spirit, …" Matthew 28:19 (NKJV). It is significant that Jesus uses the singular word "Name" not names, also He uses the definite article (the) before each individual name "the Father," "the Son," "the Holy Spirit." Oneness and Individuality or as some say, Unity and Diversity. Why did He do this?

One might ask, does the Bible teach that Jesus is deity or is He God? Most Bible students would answer yes to this question. Due to the brevity of this book, we will limit our biblical evidence to a couple of passages. Turn with me to the book of John, "In the beginning was the Word, and the Word was with God, and the Word was God." John 1:1 (NKJV)

In this verse we have the second Person in the Trinity who is referred to as the Word (Jesus), observe what John says about Him: "He was there from the beginning," "The Word was with God," and here is the clincher, "the Word was God." How much clearer can it get? All we are doing is allowing the Bible to say what it wants to say without twisting it or violating the context.

Well, how do we know that this was Jesus? Drop down to verse 14: "And the Word became flesh and dwelt among us, and we beheld His glory, the glory as of the only begotten of the Father, full of grace and truth." John 1:14 (NKJV) This is clearly making reference to the incarnation of Jesus. This is why they label Him as the "God-Man." Meaning, that He is 100% God and 100% Man. The formula for Him is one Person, two natures. He is the unique one, He has a divine and human nature.

There is a beautiful passage in the book of Hebrews that gives very strong evidence of the deity of Jesus. We will use only excerpts, so the reader is encouraged to study the entire passage in its context. In this passage, God the Father is portrayed as speaking about and to His Son. "But to the Son He says: 'Your throne, O God, is forever and ever; A scepter of righteousness is the scepter of Your kingdom. You have loved righteousness and hated lawlessness; Therefore God, Your God, has anointed You, with the oil of gladness more than Your companions.'" Hebrews 1:8,9 (NKJV)

Here we have the Father without a doubt referring to the second Person in the Trinity, His Son, as God. In our view, there can't be any stronger biblical evidence than this. It comes right out of the mouth of God.

So far, we see that the Scripture teaches that there at least two Persons that deity is ascribed to, God the Father and God the Son. As for God the Father, there are usually no questions about Him being God. So far, we have a bipartite.

To complete this Godhead, let's investigate the Holy Spirit. Does the Bible teach that He is a Person or an it? Moreover, does it teach that He is God? As to Him being a person, let's observe how Jesus references Him. Turn with me to the Gospel of John, "If you love Me, keep My commandments. And I will pray the Father, and He will give you another Helper, that He may abide with you forever, the Spirit of truth, whom the world cannot receive, because it neither sees Him, nor knows Him; but you know Him, for He dwells with you and will be in you."

"… These things I have spoken to you while being present with you. But the Helper, the Holy Spirit, whom the Father will send in My name, He will teach you all things and bring to your remembrance all things I said to you." John 14: 15,16; 25,26 (NKJV)

Take note that as Jesus is speaking about the Holy Spirit, He applies third-person pronouns "He" and "Him" to the Holy Spirit. If He is just an "it" or a "force," would He (Jesus) refer to Him in this manner? Furthermore, Jesus told His disciples that the Spirit would teach them. Does a force teach? No, the Bible consistently gives the qualities of personhood to the Holy Spirit. For example, He can teach, be grieved, be quenched, and be blasphemed.

Note what Jesus says about Him teaching: "These things I have spoken to you while being present with you. But the Helper, the Holy Spirit, whom the Father will send in My name, He will teach you all things and bring to your remembrance all that I said to you." John 14:25,26 (NKJV)

Also, the Scripture asserts that He (Holy Spirit) can be grieved, "And do not grieve the Holy Spirit of God, by whom you were sealed for the day of redemption." Ephesians 4:30 (NKJV) He can be quenched, "Do not quench the Spirit." 1 Thessalonians 5:19 (NKJV) And lastly, He can be blasphemed, let's go to Matthew's gospel, Jesus is speaking, "Therefore I say to you, every sin and blasphemy will be forgiven men, but the blasphemy against the Spirit will not be forgiven men."

"Anyone who speaks a word against the Son of Man, it will be forgiven him; but whoever speaks against the Holy Spirit, it will not be forgiven him, either in this age or in the age to come." Matthew 12:31,32 (NKJV) So we see that the Spirit is just as much a Person as is God the Father and God the Son.

Also, the Holy Spirit participates in deity as much as the other two. For instance, in the book of Acts, He is referred to as God. Let's go there: "But Peter said, 'Ananias, why has Satan filled your heart to lie to the Holy Spirit and keep back part of the price of the land for yourself? While it remained, was it not your own? And after it was sold, was it not in your own control?

Why have you conceived this thing in your heart? You have not lied to men but to God.'"

Observe closely that in this context, lying to the Holy Spirit is seen as lying to God. So, we see that the Scripture ascribes deity to the Holy Spirit. Make very sure when you read this passage that you slow down and think about what is being said. We have, in my view, scripturally argued for the Person and Deity of the Holy Spirit. Therefore, we conclude from the Bible that there is one God that exists in three Persons or one Essence that exists in three Persons. God the Father, God the Son, and God the Holy Spirit.

Many more verses could be brought to bear in support of this concept. But these will suffice. Remember, this is not taught because we fully understand it, but because it is a revealed doctrine. God took the initiative to reveal Himself in this manner. Why spend so much time discussing the nature of God in this particular subject, "Saved Forever," because we believe knowing His (God's) true nature strengthens our confidence that He will keep every promise that He has made.

For example, if He is a God that changes His mind on these important issues or does not keep His promises, then we would have to agree with that group that believes once salvation has been acquired it is possible to lose it. So, when we study from the Scripture how and what He has revealed about Himself and how He has interacted with His people in the past, making and keeping promises, this gives us strong assurance that He will not fail on any of His promises.

In this book, we appeal totally to His divine nature, a promise keeping God, a God that doesn't change His mind at the drop of a hat, a God of love, a just God, a God of compassion, a patient God, a God that is slow to anger, a God that is full of grace and mercy and a God that remembers mercy in the time of wrath.

Let's look at a specific historical case of God interacting with His ancient people. For instance, God promised Abraham, the father of the Jews, that He was going to give them a particular area of land and multiply his descendants. He made a covenant with him and swore by Himself that He would fulfill this promise. For when God made a promise to Abraham, since He had no one greater to swear by,

He swore by Himself: *"I will most certainly bless you, and I will greatly multiply you."*

And so, after waiting patiently, Abraham obtained the promise. ... Because God wanted to show His unchangeable purpose even more clearly to the heirs of the promise, He guaranteed it with an oath, so that through two unchangeable things, in which it is impossible for God to lie, Hebrews 6: 13,14,15,17,18b (HCSB)

Observe how the story unfolded with Abraham; Sarah, his wife, was barren (unable to have children). It is important to understand that the promises were given to him while she was childless. Then one day they had three strange visitors that left the following message with them: "And He said, 'I will certainly return to you according to the time of life, and behold, Sarah your wife shall have a son.'" Genesis 18:10 (NKJV)

This event would be the beginning of the fulfillment of God's promises to Abraham. The following year, Sarah would have a boy, whom they named Isaac. Isaac went on to have two boys, Esau and Jacob. God, according to His sovereign will, chose Jacob to pass on His covenant promises to. Important to understand that it was not because of Jacob's righteousness that he was chosen, but the sovereign grace of God. From Jacob's two wives and their handmaids would derive twelve sons and one recorded daughter, thus, we have the twelve tribes of Israel.

Since God kept His promises to Abraham, we should have all the confidence in the world that He is going to keep His promises to us. This should give those who are truly Jesus' sheep the utmost assurance that when Jesus says, "My sheep will never ever perish," He means just that. They are eternally secure!

Moreover, the prophet Malachi depicts God as saying He doesn't change. "For I am the LORD, I do not change; Therefore, you are not consumed, O sons of Jacob." Malachi 3:6 (NKJV)

In our own experiences, as saved sinners, are we in the habit of giving someone a gift, then changing our minds and asking for its return? Not hardly. How much more, God being perfect, will His gift of salvation remain secure.

I am mindful of a very interesting passage in the Gospel of Luke that is relevant here. Jesus is speaking: "If a son asks for bread from any father among you, will he give him a stone? Or if he asks for a fish, will he give him a serpent instead of a fish? Or if he asks for an egg, will he offer him a scorpion? If you then, being evil, know how to give good gifts to your children, how much more will your heavenly Father give the Holy Spirit to those who ask Him!" Luke 11:11-13 (NKJV) If the Father gives, will He take it back?

CHAPTER 2

WHAT IS BIBLICAL SALVATION?

It is important to understand that the general term "salvation" has multiple meanings.

As always, the meaning of a word is derived from the context in which it is used. So, it is with this one. For example, there are multiple dictionaries that give the meaning of the word salvation as "deliverance." So, when it is used scripturally from a Christian perspective, it usually means, spiritually deliverance, that is, from sin.

For instance, Dr. Tatmon, in his book *Doctrine Still Matters*, quotes the following from Dr. Barackman:

"Its Biblical Description: Essentially, salvation is a deliverance. To save is to rescue or deliver someone from calamity, loss, or destruction. Its Secular Meaning: Secular salvation is a deliverance from some natural or physical danger or affliction (Exod. 14:30; Ps. 34:6). Its Spiritual Meaning: Spiritual salvation is deliverance from the ruin, guilt, and debt of our sins as well as from bondage to our spiritual enemies and their works in our lives. These spiritual enemies are the sin force, Satan, and the world of unsaved people (Eph. 2:1-10)."

Something critical happened to humankind to warrant its need of a spiritual deliverance.

In order to fully understand this, one must return to the beginnings, which are contained in the book of Genesis. Here we observe the creation of all things by the hand of God. Let's do some excerpts from this book. Turn with me to the first chapter of Genesis. "In the beginning God created the heavens and the earth." It is noteworthy that some scholars consider this as a summary statement, where Moses tells us what He (God) did, whereas the following verses tell us how He did it. For example, Dr. H.L. Willmington states this: "This is a summarization statement, 1:1 Tells us what God did. 1:2-2:25 Tells us how He did it."

As we know, God created everything within a six-day period, including His crowning creation, Adam and Eve. The Bible asserts that God gave Adam certain instructions, chief among them being the following: "Then the LORD God took the man and put him in the garden of Eden to tend and keep it. And the LORD God commanded the man, saying, 'Of every tree of the garden you may freely eat; but of the knowledge of good and evil you shall not eat, for in the day that you eat or it you shall surely die.'" Genesis 2:15-17 (NKJV)

Apparently, Eve had not arrived on the scene yet when Adam received this information. But God gave very clear instructions to Adam concerning what he was permitted to do and not to do. Many scholars and theologians are of the mindset that Adam passed on these instructions to Eve as well. This would leave no room for the plead of ignorance, that is, saying I didn't know.

As time passed, they found themselves at the forbidden tree, violating the holiness of God. We find the history of this in Genesis chapter 3: The scene opens with the serpent dialoguing with Eve, "Now the serpent was more cunning than any beast of the field which the LORD God had made. And he said to the woman, "Has God indeed said, 'You shall not eat of every tree of the garden'?"

And the woman said to the serpent, "We may eat the fruit of the trees of the garden; but of the fruit of the tree, which is in the midst of the garden, God has said, 'You shall not eat it, nor shall you touch it, lest you die.'"

It appears that Eve may have added something to God's instructions: 'Nor shall you touch it.' Remember, the Bible warns us about adding or taking away from God's word. Case and point, "For I testify to everyone who hears the words of the prophecy of this book: If anyone adds to these things, God will add to him the plagues that are written in this book; and if anyone takes away from the words of the book of this prophecy, God shall take away his part from the Book of Life..." Revelation 22: 18,19a (NKJV)

Meanwhile, the serpent continues: "Then the serpent said to the woman, 'You will not surely die. For God knows that in the day you eat of it your eyes will be opened, and you will be like God, knowing good and evil.'"

Take note, it appears that during this dialogue session, the serpent blatantly contradicts God. God said, "...the day you eat, you will die." The serpent tells Eve, "You shall not surely die."

Currently, in our society, we are in the midst of objective truth being denied. Many have succumbed to a very popular theory known as "relativism." Simply stated, it asserts, "Your truth is your truth and my truth is my truth." It vehemently rejects the idea of absolute truth. In many circles of our current society, contradictions are not frowned upon. Matter of fact about it, some even consider them to be deep truths. Not so with God! You can be certain that He frowns upon such nonsense!

We are indebted to Dr. R.C. Sproul for shedding light on the term "contradiction." Contradiction comes from the Latin *contra-* is the prefix, which means "against"; literally, a contradiction is speaking against something.

Dr. Sproul continues by contrasting "mystery vs. contradiction." Mystery involves a lack of understanding or an absence of knowledge. If there is any point of contact between contradiction and mystery, it is this: both contradictions and mysteries are not understood at present. But one important difference remains: contradictions can never be understood—they are inherently unintelligible. Even God cannot understand a contradiction. For God, there is no such thing as a square circle. However, in time, with the gaining of more information, what is a mystery now may be revealed.

On a side note, don't follow in Eve's train (not only her) don't dialogue with the Devil; talk to Jesus!

"So when the woman saw that the tree was good for food, that it was pleasant to the eyes, and a tree desirable to make one wise, she took of its fruit and ate. She also gave to her husband with her, and he ate."

"Then the eyes of both of them were opened, and they knew that they were naked; and they sewed fig leaves together and made themselves coverings." Genesis 3: 1-7 (NKJV)

It is imperative that we understand where it all began. Keep in mind that all the human race was in the loins of Adam and Eve. Because they represented all of humanity, their fall and failure were imputed to every human being that would come upon the face of the earth. The only exception to this would be Jesus the Christ, the unique One.

According to the Apostle Paul, all have sinned and fallen short of the glory of God. Furthermore, in Romans, Paul says this: "Therefore, just as through one man sin entered the world, and death through sin, and thus death spread to all men, because all sinned.

"...But the free gift is not like the offense. For if by the one man's offense many died, much more the grace of God and the gift by the grace of one Man, Jesus Christ, abound to many.

"...For as by one man's disobedience many were made sinners, so also by one man's obedience many will be made righteous." Romans 5:12, 15, 19 (NKJV) It is because of what happened in the garden that everyone needs to be saved from their sins. Just as Paul says, "All have sinned."

Moreover, it is vitally significant that we understand that one cannot save himself or herself! We need an outside entity to provide this salvation. Take note that after Adam and Eve sinned, they attempted to cover their nakedness with fig leaves (a picture of mankind trying to provide salvation for themselves). This was not acceptable to God, so He stepped in by His grace, (Grace and Gift highlighted above) and provided a skin covering for them, which would obviously involve the shedding of blood of an innocent animal. Only God can save.

Interesting that the Bible says, "Without the shedding of blood, there is no remission of sins." This act looked far out into the future and saw John the Baptist proclaiming, "Behold the Lamb of God who takes away the sin of the world." This is making reference to Jesus of Nazareth.

It is very important that one is aware of this background in order to fully understand why we need spiritual salvation or deliverance from the bondage of our sins that came into the world through our fore parents, Adam and Eve.

CHAPTER 3

JESUS THE CHRIST

The Apostle Paul asserts in the book of Galatians, "But when the fullness of the time had come, God sent forth His Son, born of a woman, born under the law, to redeem those who were under the law, that we might receive the adoption as sons." Galatians 4:4,5 (NKJV)

It was according to God's timing that Jesus entered the world, not coincidence, not by so-called chance. Since God is sovereign, He is totally in control of all things, even time. It's interesting that God the Father didn't leave it to humans to select a name for His Son, Jesus.

Let's go to Matthew's Gospel, "But while he thought about these things, behold, an angel of the Lord appeared to him in a dream, saying, 'Joseph, son of David, do not be afraid to take to you Mary your wife, for that which is conceived in her is of the Holy Spirit. And she will bring forth a Son, and you shall call His name Jesus, for He will save His people from their sins.'" Matthew 1:20,21 (NKJV)

Here the author gives us the reason that His name would be called Jesus, "…for He shall save His people from their sins." Notice the author didn't say, make it possible to be saved or saved for a limited amount of time.

There is an interesting verse in the book of Hebrews that we believe to be relevant at this point, "Therefore He is also able to save to the uttermost those who come to God through Him, since He always lives to make intercession for them." Hebrews 7:25 (NKJV)

In our view, we believe that this is one of the strongest verses in the Bible that supports the security of the saint's salvation once he or she is truly saved. Observe closely what the author is saying, first he says, He, meaning Jesus, is able to save to the uttermost, to the greatest degree, anyone that comes to God through Him (Jesus). Second, since He, meaning Jesus, resides in heaven at the right-hand side of the Father making intercession for them always. Let me ask this question. Will there ever be a time when any of Jesus' prayers go unanswered? We believe the answer to this question is an emphatic no!

Remember the following event just before Jesus completed His earthly ministry concerning Peter: "And the Lord said, Simon, Simon! Indeed, Satan has asked for you, that he may sift you as wheat. But I have prayed for you, that your faith should not fail; and when you have returned to Me, strengthen your brethren." Matthew 22:31,32 (NKJV)

What a verse! Isn't it noteworthy that Satan had to ask to sift Peter as wheat? Why didn't Satan just do it? Why ask permission? Reminds me of his (Satan's) encounter with Job, there Satan noted that God had a protective fence around Job and that he could only get at him if God removed it. Note Satan dialoguing with God, "So Satan answered the LORD and said, 'Does Job fear God for nothing? Have You not made a hedge around him, around his household, and around all that he has on every side?

"…But now, stretch out Your hand and touch all that he has, and he will surely curse You to Your face!"

"And the LORD said to Satan, 'Behold, all that he has is in your power; only do not lay a hand on his person.'" Job 1:10b,11,12b (NKJV) What's happening here? Satan's desire is to get to Job, but he can't until God allows it, and even when God allows it, his (Satan) control is limited! What a comfort!

Jesus assured Peter that He would pray for him. Note that Jesus didn't say "if" you come back to Me, but "when" you return. It's very comforting to know that Jesus' prayers are always answered. This goes to the very heart of our argument for eternal security. That as long as Jesus is interceding for the saints, they will never ever lose their salvation. They will endure until the end! How long will He intercede? For all eternity!

Come with me to another intriguing passage of Scripture that is pertinent to this point, in the Gospel of John. Many scholars refer to this passage as Jesus' great high priestly prayer. Notice that He prays for Himself, His Apostles, and future believers. We will look at a few excerpts, observing the terms "give," "given," and "gave" in this section.

The Father is portrayed as giving Jesus various ones. "Father, the hour has come. Glorify Your Son, that Your Son also may glorify You, as You have given Him authority over all flesh, that He should give eternal life to as many as You have given Him. And this is eternal life, that they may know You, the only true God, and Jesus Christ whom You have sent. I have glorified You on the earth. I have finished the work which You have given Me to do. And now, O Father, glorify Me together with Yourself, with the glory which I had with You before the world was." John 17:1b-5 (NKJV)

Observe closely as we call attention to numerous things that are in this passage.

First, Jesus asserts that His Father had given Him authority over all flesh, then He said something quite interesting. That "He" Jesus, should give eternal life to as many as the "Father" had given. Who is the giver? The Father. Who is the recipient? Jesus. Who are the ones given? In this immediate context, it is His disciples that He will pray for shortly, as well as many in the future who will believe and receive the gospel message that will be preached.

Now, what kind of life is He giving them? Eternal life or temporary life? It is imperative that we allow the Bible to say what it wants to say and then accept what it says. Here we have it saying that those given to Jesus will receive eternal life! Remember, sound doctrine is to be built on clear passages, not vague or doubtful ones. We don't think that there is any ambiguity about what's being said here.

Again, we have Jesus mentioning in prayer: "I pray for them. I do not pray for the world but for those whom You have given Me, for they are Yours. And all Mine are Yours, and Yours are Mine, and I am glorified in them." John 17: 9,10 (NKJV)

Jesus explicitly states that He is not praying for the world, but for those who have been given to Him. In other words, He is not praying for those who are not His. As He continues, He says the following, "...While I was with them in the world, I kept them in Your name. Those whom You gave Me I have kept; and none of them is lost except the son of perdition, that the Scripture might be fulfilled." John 17:12 (NKJV)

At the risk of being repetitive, will the prayers of Jesus fail in respect to the saint's security during this current period?

Observe the last group that Jesus prays for, "I do not pray for these alone, but also for those who will believe in Me through their word;" John 17: 20a, (NKJV) I think it's safe to say that you and I are in this group, providing that we have trusted Him as our Savior. So what does this mean? It means that I am wrapped safely in His prayers!

Note Jesus states explicitly that all that the Father gave Him wasn't lost. Why? Because He kept them! Is He able to keep us until the end? I am convinced by the clear testimony of the Scripture that He absolutely can and will.

The following passage is another very powerful Scripture for the doctrine of eternal security. In our opinion, if the following passage was the only one available to us, it would be sufficient to support the subject of once saved, always saved. Watch closely what Jesus is saying: "Jesus answered them, 'I told you, and you do not believe. The works that I do in My Father's name, they bear witness of Me. But you do not believe, because you are not My sheep, as I said to you. My sheep hear My voice, and I know them, and they follow Me. And I give them eternal life, and they shall never perish; neither shall anyone snatch them out of My hand. My Father, who has given them to Me, is greater than all; and no one is able to snatch them out of My Father's hand. I and My Father are one.'" John 10:25-30 (NKJV)

Here He states emphatically that some in the audience were not His sheep (most likely the religious Jews). Then He goes on to talk about those that are His sheep. Notice the contrast: those who are not His sheep don't know or hear His voice. However, those who are His, recognize His voice. Without a doubt, they will follow Him. Furthermore, He says they will never ever perish. Why? Because they are in His all-powerful hands, and if this wasn't enough, they are in His Father's Hands. Watch closely; nothing and no one can get to His sheep! There might be someone who says, "That's true, however, I can jump out."

First, if you are truly His why would you want to leap out of His hands? Second, are you strong enough to break the grip of both of those hands plus the Seal of the Holy Spirit? Tell me, how much more secure can one get? Again, we can't emphasize enough that if one is truly born again, his or her salvation is secure forevermore.

Finally, we will look at one more passage that Jesus brings forth on this subject: "All that the Father gives Me will come to Me, and the one who comes to Me I will by no means cast out. For I have come down from heaven, not to do My own will, but the will of Him who sent Me. This is the will of the Father who sent Me, that of all He has given Me I should lose nothing but should raise it up at the last day. And this is the will of Him who sent Me, that everyone who sees the Son and believes in Him may have everlasting life; and I will raise him up at the last day." John 6:37-40 (NKJV)

Take note again, Jesus says all that the Father has given Him will come to Him, not might, but will come. Moreover, He tells His audience that those who come to Him will not be cast out. He further says that He is not going to lose any. Some think that God gave us the gift of salvation and left it up to us to hold on to it the best we can. Do we know how long we would remain saved if He did this? No quicker than a cat can wink its eye!

One of the questions that comes to my mind is, how much sin does a believer have to commit to lose his or her salvation? One? Two? One hundred? Or one thousand? Please raise your hand if you know the answer!

Here, we want to be very careful, because the Enemy will try to twist the point that is trying to be made. Be mindful that no genuine believer is going to be comfortable practicing sin on a continuous basis. The emphasis is on the term "comfortable."

There is a saying: you can wash a pig, clean him up really nicely. The moment you release him, he will head for the first mud hole that can be found to wallow in. Now let's not be too hard on the pig. He is just following his nature; he loves mud. On the other hand, you can clean a sheep up, and if he should by chance fall into the mud, he will attempt to get out; he doesn't like wallowing in the mud. Why? Because he is a sheep. He has a different nature from a pig.

What's the point?

A truly born-again believer will sometimes fall into mud (sin); however, because he or she has a new nature, their desires have changed. Paul is helpful here, "If anyone is in Christ, he is a new creation; old things have passed away; behold, all things have become new." 2 Corinthians 5:17 (NKJV)

Moreover, the Holy Spirit will make sure that he or she is as uncomfortable as possible in that mud hole, to the point that, by the grace of God, a genuine believer gets out (confesses and repents) and continues his walk with the Lord. Remember, grace is not a license to sin. It seems as if the apostle Paul was attempting to address this same thing to the Church at Rome. "What shall we say then? Shall we continue in sin that grace may abound? Certainly not! How shall we who died to sin live any longer in it?"

"…Therefore do not let sin reign in your mortal body, that you should obey it in its lust." Romans 6:1,2,12 (NKJV)

It is significant to understand that as Christians our obedience emerges from the love that we have for God. And even this is placed there by the Holy Spirit. For example, Paul says, "Now hope does not disappoint, because the love of God has been poured out in our hearts by the Holy Spirit who was given to us." Romans 5:5 (NKJV)

CHAPTER 4

THE ROLE OF THE HOLY SPIRIT

We have previously argued for the deity and personhood of the Holy Spirit; this will not be repeated. We will only reiterate that according to the Scripture He is not a force and should not be referred to as an "it."

His role is multifaceted. First, He regenerates:

> "But when the kindness and love of God our Savior toward man appeared, not by works of righteousness which we have done, but according to His mercy He saved us, through the washing of regeneration and renewing of the Holy Spirit whom He poured out on us

abundantly through Jesus Christ our Savior, that having been justified by His grace we should become heirs according to the hope of eternal life." Titus 3:47 (NKJV)

So regeneration is part of the Holy Spirit's ministry.

John 3 is a very familiar passage for many. Let's go there. Here we have Jesus' night session with a religious ruler named Nicodemus. What really arrested Nicodemus' attention were the signs that Jesus was performing. "Rabbi, we know that You are a teacher come from God; for no one can do these signs that You do unless God is with him." John 3b (NKJV)

Notice Jesus' response to him: "Jesus answered and said to him, 'Most assuredly, I say to you, unless one is born again, he cannot see the kingdom of God."

Nicodemus is confused and perplexed about Jesus' response, and asked, "How can a man be born when he is old?"

This gives Jesus the opportunity to explain this new "birth" to him:

"Most assuredly, I say to you, unless one is born of water and the Spirit, he cannot enter the kingdom of God. That which is born of the flesh is flesh, and that which is born of the Spirit is spirit. Do not marvel that I said to you, 'You must be born again.' The wind blows where it wishes, and you hear the sound of it, but cannot tell where it comes from and where it goes. So is everyone who is born of the Spirit." John 3: 5-8 (NKJV)

The point that we would like to highlight is that the Holy Spirit is involved in this new birth, "born of the Spirit." He regenerates. As we continue to read this passage, we see that Jesus says, those that believe will not perish.

Let's go to the 16th verse: "For God so loved the world that He gave His only begotten Son, that whoever believes in Him should not perish but have everlasting life." What kind of life? Everlasting life!

Moreover, it is very interesting and comforting to know that the Holy Spirit is described as being our seal. For example, the book of Ephesians asserts this, "In Him you also trusted, after you heard the word of truth, the gospel of your salvation; in whom also, having believed, you were sealed with the Holy Spirit of promise, who is the guarantee of our inheritance until the redemption of the purchased possession, to the praise of His glory." Ephesians 1:13,14 (NKJV)

Moreover, the Apostle taught the Church at Corinth, "…who also has sealed us and given us the Spirit in our hearts as a guarantee." 2 Corinthians 1:22 (NKJV)

Observe the progression: they heard the word (Gospel), they believed it, which led to them trusting Jesus as their Savior. At this junction, the Holy Spirit sealed them; pay close attention to where it says He (the Holy Spirit) is the guarantee of our inheritance. What does guarantee mean? According to Dictionary.com, "The legal definition of guarantee is an assurance that something will be fulfilled as intended."

Kevin DeYoung gives us some insight from his site: "Ephesians 1:13-14 states, that in Christ we 'were sealed with the promised Holy Spirit, who is the guarantee of our inheritance until we acquire possession of it.'

"A seal in the ancient world did three things: it authenticated, it secured, and it marked ownership. All three elements are probably in view here. The seal of the Spirit authenticates us as true believers, secures our eternal safety, and marks us out as belonging to God."

This reminds us of a passage in the letter written to the Philippians, "Being confident of this very thing, that He who has begun a good work in you will complete it until the day of Jesus Christ." Philippians 1:6 (NKJV)

One can be sure that God doesn't begin something and doesn't finish it.

CHAPTER 5

THE APOSTLES' VIEW

What was the mindset of some of the apostles on this subject? Although the form of the question is not stated as we have it, we can be certain that they believed in the security of our salvation from the material that they wrote.

Many of us are aware that the Apostle Paul wrote most of the New Testament letters. We believe it is safe to say that he was a strong advocate of the security of the salvation of the saints. For instance, he records the following:

> "What then shall we say to these things? If God is for us, who can be against us? He who

did not spare His own Son, but delivered Him up for us all, how shall He not with Him also freely give us all things? Who shall bring a charge against God's elect? Who is he who condemns? It is Christ who died, and furthermore is also risen, who is even at the right hand of God, who also makes intercession for us. Who shall separate us from the love of Christ? Shall tribulation, or distress, or persecution, or famine, or nakedness, or peril, or sword?" Romans 8:31-35 (NKJV)

Please read through this passage very slowly, allowing what the Apostle is saying to settle in our minds and hearts. How do we know that God is for us? Because He sent His Son to die for us. Therefore, we know that no one and nothing can stand successfully against us.

Furthermore, he says, who can bring a charge against God's elect? The obvious answer is no one! Why? Because Christ's death, burial and resurrection took care of this. Lastly, he asked his audience, "Who shall separate us from the love of Christ?" Then he goes on and lists a few things that cannot separate us. This is not an exhaustive list.

Those who hold to the view that one can lose his or her salvation after being genuinely saved have to grapple with this passage. Paul, under the guidance of the Holy Spirit, emphatically states that *nothing* can separate us from the love of Christ! We can't emphasize enough, "when one is genuinely saved."

Furthermore, the Apostle Peter picks up on this term "elect" in his first letter. Turn with me to his letter: "…elect according to the foreknowledge of God the Father, sanctification of the Spirit, for obedience and sprinkling of the blood of Jesus Christ.

"…who are kept by the power of God through faith for salvation ready to be revealed in the last time." 1 Peter 1:2,5 (NKJV)

It is noteworthy to observe that God knew who we were before we arrived on Earth and chose us according to His sovereign grace. Even when we were in the womb, listen to David: "For You formed my inward parts; You covered me in my mother's womb… Your eyes saw my substance, being yet unformed. And in Your book, they all were written..." Psalm 139:13, 16c (NKJV)

Isn't this comforting to know that God was watching over us in the womb? How secure is this?

Also, Peter continues on and says, "...they were 'kept' by the power of God." This reminds me of a verse in the book of Zechariah where it says, "...not by might nor by power, but by My Spirit, says the LORD of hosts." Zechariah 4:6

You see, when one receives Jesus as his or her personal Savior, the Spirit comes and lives inside of him or her; He is the one that ultimately keeps us, by His divine power. Not our power!

The following concept might be helpful at this point. We will borrow the following idea from previous scholars, which is known as the "Three P's," meaning: (1) Penalty (2) Power and (3) Present. We think that this will give us a better idea of what really happened in God's salvation plan.

First, "Penalty," (Justification) what do we mean by penalty within the context of spiritual salvation? Turn with me to a passage in Romans: "But now having been set free from sin, and having become slaves of God, you have your fruit to holiness, and the end, everlasting life. For the wages of sin is death, but the gift of God is eternal life in Christ Jesus our Lord." Romans 6: 22, 23 (NKJV)

As we can observe, there is a penalty for sin, which according to Paul is death. In theology, the term death oftentimes means "separation." For example, when the spirit and soul are separated from the body, physical death occurs.

Observe the following verse in the Epistle of James. He asserts this, "For as the body without the spirit is dead, so faith without works is dead also." James 2:26 (NKJV)

Moreover, spiritual death means that mankind has been separated from God because of sin. The prophet Isaiah is helpful here, "…But your Iniquities have separated you from your God; And your sins have hidden His face from you, So that He will not hear." Isaiah 59: 2 (NKJV)

Furthermore, the apostle Paul weighs in with this figurative language, "And you He made alive, who were dead in trespasses and sins, …even when we were dead in trespasses, made us alive together with Christ (by grace you have been saved)." Ephesians 2: 1,5 (NKJV)

Lastly, eternal death is where mankind is eternally separated from God because he rejected God's salvation plan. Apostle John refers to this as the second death: "Then Death and Hades were cast into the lake of fire. This is the second death. Revelation 21:14 (NKJV)

This is where God's Son, Jesus the Christ, enters. It is very important to understand that mankind needed a perfect substitute for his sins, which immediately exempted any human being on the planet. For the Bible states that "All have sinned and come short of the glory of God." However, there was one human being that would come on the scene who was perfect, Jesus, the only begotten of the Father. This One participated both in deity and humanity. He is referred to by scholars and theologians as, the God-Man, meaning 100% God and 100% Man, the unique One. He is the Lamb that takes away our sins. His death completely and fully paid the penalty for all our sins: past, present, and future.

When we refer to the "Power" of sins, we are addressing our everyday walk with God. (Sanctification) Because if we have been truly born again, the Holy Spirit resides in our bodies and gives us the power to resist temptation and sins on a daily basis. And when we fall short, and we surely will, He will convict and convince us to repent.

Many scholars believe the Apostle Paul is addressing this issue in Romans as well, "Knowing this, that our old man was crucified with Him, that the body of sin might be done away with, that we should no longer be slaves of sin. For he who has died has been freed from sin. Therefore do not let sin reign in your mortal body, that you should obey it in its lusts." Romans 6:6,7,12 (NKJV)

So we are able to resist the power of sin daily, as we yield to the Holy Spirit.

Finally, someday in the future we will be out of the very "Presence" of sin (Glorification). This will happen when we receive our glorified bodies. In 1 John 3, this is stated, "Beloved, now we are children of God; and it has not yet been revealed what we shall be, but we know that when He is revealed, we shall be like Him, for we shall see Him as He is." 1 John 3:2 (NKJV)

Moreover, Philippians adds to this, "...who will transform our lowly body that it may be conformed to His glorious body, according to the working by which He is able even to subdue all things to Himself." Philippians 3:21 (NKJV) I am convinced that all of us long for this day to be saved from the very presence of sin.

We believe that the Bible teaches that we have been justified, sanctified, and eventually will be glorified. This is another way to look at the Three Ps.

Let us return to the book of Ephesians and interact with an important passage in the first chapter. This is one of Paul's prison Epistles, we will begin after his salutations and greetings,1-2, with verse 3:

> "Blessed be the God and Father of our Lord Jesus Christ, who has blessed us with every spiritual blessing in heavenly places in Christ, just as He chose us in Him before the foundation of the world, that we should be holy and without blame before Him in love, having predestined us to adoption as sons by

> Jesus Christ to Himself, according to the good pleasure of His will, to the praise of the glory of His grace, by which He made us accepted in the beloved. In Him we have redemption through His blood, the forgiveness of sins, according to the riches of His grace..." Ephesians 1:4-7 (NKJV)

I cannot truly understand how one can read this passage and afterwards conclude that he or she can lose their salvation. First, observe what the Apostle Paul says to this church at Ephesus and, by extension, to us who are saved.

Read it slowly: He (God the Father) chose us in Him, (Jesus) before the foundation of the world. Just stop and meditate on this for about seven days! In God's mind, everything was settled at that point: we were as good as in Heaven! Moreover, pay close attention to the multiple prepositional phrases that the Apostle uses in reference to Jesus, particularly, "In Him," also, "in Christ," and "In the Beloved," which speaks of Jesus as well. Moreover, we think it's noteworthy that the Apostle uses the term "good pleasure" twice in this passage. Why did God choose, call, and save us? We are convinced, because of His good pleasure.

He does it because it pleases Him! Be reminded, it is because of God's good pleasure that these things are being done. Be sure to read this chapter in its entirety.

To us the following passage is fascinating, "...even when we were dead in trespasses, made us alive together with Christ (by grace you have been saved), and raised us up together, and made us sit together in the heavenly places in Christ Jesus, that in the ages to come He might show the exceeding riches of His grace in His kindness toward us in Christ Jesus." Ephesians 2:5,6,7 (NKJV)

Paul emphasized to them that they had been saved by the grace of God, which is a gift from Him. He further tells them that they have been seated together with Him (Jesus) in heavenly places. How secure is this?

Moreover, in his letter to the Colossians (which is also another prison Epistle) he asserts the following:

> "If then you were raised with Christ, seek those things which are above, where Christ is, sitting at the right hand of God. Set your mind on things above, not on things on the earth. For you died, and your life is hidden with Christ in God. When Christ who is our life appears, then

you also will appear with Him in glory." Colossians 3:1-4 (NKJV)

Observe the Apostle as he says, our life is hidden with Christ in God. Question—if it is hidden, can anyone find it? Including the Devil, demons, or even ourselves? How much more secure can we get?

Furthermore, the disciple Jude asserts this: "Now to Him who is able to keep you from stumbling, and to present you faultless, Before the presence of His glory with exceeding joy." Jude 1 (NKJV)

Jude assures his audience that God is able to keep them from stumbling. He goes a step further and says that He (God) will present them faultless before His presence. What a salvation we have! Aren't you glad that it doesn't depend on you for its security?

CHAPTER 6

PAST CENTURIES THEOLOGIANS

There are many theologians and scholars who have come and gone who have composed certain theological systems for better or worse. We will limit our study to just a few that have made a significant impact in the history of the Church, which are John Calvin, Jacobus Arminius, Charles Hodge, Alfred Edersheim, and Charles Spurgeon.

In our opinion, we think that it would benefit many in the Christian community to at least familiarize themselves with the contrasting systems of Calvin and Arminius, whether we agree with them or not.

Familiarity with them may shed a glimmer of light as to why many Christians believe that one can lose his or her salvation.

First, we will briefly observe John Calvin's system. GotQuestion.com, states the following: "John Calvin (1509-1564) was a French theologian who was instrumental in the Protestant Reformation and who continues to hold wide influence today in theology, education, and even politics."

Calvin is known largely for his great work. Gotquestions.com asserts this: "Calvin's theological magnum opus, *Institutes of the Christian Religion*, was originally intended to explain biblical doctrine in a systematic way."

Moreover, the Calvinists are well known for their use of the acronym "TULIP" to explain the five points of Calvinism, which we will also use.

Total Depravity

Got Questions states this: "Every part of man-his mind, will, emotions and flesh have been corrupted by sin. In other words, sin affects all areas of our being including who we are and what we do. It penetrates to the very core of our being so that everything is tainted by sin '…all our acts are like filthy rages' before a holy God." (Isaiah 64:6)

Unconditional Election

Meaning that there are no conditions attached to the Election of God. According to Erwin Lutzer, "The synod affirmed that the reason some are saved is because God elected them to eternal life; others are condemned to eternal death. Because salvation rests wholly with God, no one can say he chose Christ because he is wiser than others; he did so because God had chosen him that he might believe."

Limited Atonement

Also, is referred to as Particular Atonement, meaning that Christ died only for the Elect, that is, for a particular people. Gotquestions.com weighs in with, "'Limited atonement' is a term that is used to summarize what the Bible teaches about the purpose for Christ's death on the cross and what His life, death and resurrection accomplished."

Irresistible Grace

Erwin again gives us some insight: "Calvinist, in my opinion, should drop this phrase and substitute 'efficacious or effectual grace.' This phrase means simply that when God applies his saving grace to the elect, it is always effective." In our view, it assures us that God will not fail in what He sets out to do, to save those who are truly His.

Perseverance of the Saints

"This doctrine is the logical outcome of the preceding tenets of Calvinism. Historically, it means that the saints will persevere in their faith. None of the elect will be lost," states Erwin.

Now that we have completed the Calvinist section, we will move on to those that historically opposed it. Jacobus Arminius being chief among them, and later those that held to his point of view, namely, the Remonstrants. They exercised their disagreement with Calvinism by composing what is known as the five Articles of Remonstrance.

Again, Erwin is helpful through his brief itemization of the Arminius five Articles:

1. God decreed to save all who believe and persevere in the faith; all others are left in sin and damnation.

2. Christ died for all men, "so that he has obtained for them all, by his death on the cross, redemption and forgiveness of sins; yet that no one actually enjoys this forgiveness of sins except the believer."

3. Man has not saving grace of himself, nor of the energy of his free will "inasmuch as he, in the state of apostasy and sin, can of and by himself neither think, will, or do anything that is truly good…but that he be born again of God in Christ."

4. Without the operation of grace, man cannot do anything good, but grace is not irresistible since men have resisted The Holy Spirit."

5. Believers partake of eternal life and have power to strive against Satan. However, whether they can fall away and be lost is a matter "that must be more particularly determined out of Holy Scripture before we ourselves can teach it the full persuasion of our minds."

It would be fair to say that some scholars are of the opinion that Jacobus Arminius wasn't conclusive as to whether a believer could lose his or her salvation. Furthermore, some state that this came afterwards through the teaching of his followers.

Gotquestions.com amplifies the above point under the heading of "The possibility of falling from grace."

"In this fifth article, the Remonstrants did not utterly reject the idea of eternal security but admitted the need for further study, although it was later adopted as an established doctrine. Calvinists hold firmly to belief in the 'perseverance of the saints,' meaning a person who is elected by God will continue in faith and will not permanently deny Christ or turn away from Him. The Remonstrants affirmed that believers are empowered to live a vicious life but also concede the possibility that a person might exercise his or her own free will to turn away from Christ and lose salvation."

Another prominent scholar who appeared on the scene during the 1700s was Charles Hodge. According to some sources, he affirmed the doctrine of the perseverance of the saints. Today, this is referred to as "eternal security." A Google search provided a quote: "He taught that true believers, once regenerated by God's grace, will certainly persevere in their faith and be eternally saved. This security, however, is not based on the believer's own strength but on the immutable purpose of God."

In his *Systematic Theology*, Hodge established the basis for this position. The following will be a few selected items from his theology:

Divine Election and Covenant

He viewed perseverance as a logical necessity that follows from God's sovereign decree of election and the covenant of grace. Since God chose his people from eternity and gave them to his Son as a reward, their salvation is certain.

Christ's Atonement

Hodge taught that Christ's death was sufficient for all but efficient only for the elect. If one of the elect could fail, it would mean that the foundation of Christ's work was shaken.

Indwelling of the Holy Spirit

The Holy Spirit's presence in a believer is a seal and an earnest (or down payment) of their future redemption. This guarantees that God will complete the work he started.

God's Immutable Love

The primary foundation for security is God's eternal and unchangeable love. According to Hodge, the believer's perseverance is not dependent on their own constant will, but on the power of God, who will not allow his people to be separated from his love.

A Contrast with Mere Belief

Hodge did not argue that every person who merely claims to believe will be saved. True, saving faith is demonstrated by a life of persistent, though imperfect, holiness.

Alfred Edersheim, in the 1800s, who is very well known for his book, *The Life and Times of Jesus the Messiah,* reportedly approached this question from the standpoint of the term, "perseverance," which many others had previously done.

In his book, Edersheim addressed the possibility of believers falling into sin, as seen in the life of the Apostle Peter. He concluded that not every sin leads to the "final rejection" of a believer. Two key theories are listed below:

1. In his book, he described Peter's fall as a momentary expression of his "natural elements."

2. The purpose of Peter's fall was to remove these elements and ultimately strengthen his faith, fitting him "the better for confirming his brethren."

Edersheim's support of perseverance stems from his belief in salvation by grace through faith.

Another theologian to cover is Charles Spurgeon. The following are selected excerpts from Spurgeon, as Sam Storm has recorded them:

> "If one dear saint of God had perished, so might all; if one of the covenant ones be lost, so may all be; and then there is no gospel promise true, but the Bible is a lie, and there is nothing in it worthy my acceptance. I will be an infidel at once when I can believe that a saint of God can ever fall finally.
>
> I don't know how some people, who believe that a Christian can fall from grace, manage to be happy. It must be a very commendable thing

in them to be able to go through a day without despair. If I did not believe the doctrine of the final perseverance of the saints, I think I should be of all men the most miserable, because I should lack any ground of comfort…"

It is imperative that one remembers that salvation is a gift. The very moment that one forgets or rejects this, he or she spirals into the abyss of uncertainty and fear of losing their salvation! What kind of good news is this!

CHAPTER 7

CONTEMPORARY THEOLOGIANS

We have briefly explored the positions of past theologians concerning eternal security.

As we move forward, we will observe numerous current scholar's school of thought on this issue. A number of these theologians have recently passed on, for example, Dr. R.C. Sproul, Dr. John MacArthur, Dr. Charles Stanley, Dr. Billy Graham who died in 2018, Dr. Voddie Baucham, Dr. J. I Packer, Dr. Ron Rhodes, Dr. Robert Jefferess, Dr. David Jeremiah, and H. Wayne House.

Dr. Sproul, who was an excellent theologian and teacher, was of the persuasion that the saints were eternal secured, that is, once saved, always saved.

At this junction, Dr. Sproul weighs in:

> "The idea of the perseverance of the saints is distinguished from the assurance of salvation, though it can never be separated from it. There are those Christians in church history who have affirmed that a Christian can have assurance of his salvation, but that his assurance is only for the moment. One can know that he is in a state of grace today, but with that knowledge, or assurance, there is no further guarantee that he will remain in that state of grace tomorrow or the day after tomorrow, or unto death. On the other hand, those who believe in the perseverance of the saints believe also that one can have the assurance of salvation, not only today, but forever. So again, we see that perseverance is distinguished from assurance but can never be divorced from it."

Dr. Sproul continues, "…God's divine decree of election is not to make salvation a temporary possession of the elect but to make that salvation a permanent reality for those whom He predestines unto salvation. Again, predestination is not unto part-time, or temporary faith but unto full-time and permanent faith.

In John MacArthur's mind, a true believer is absolutely secure in his or her salvation. Note the following excerpt from his material:

> "And when you want to affirm the doctrine of security there are two passages that I would recommend to you that are unanswerable. John 10 and Romans 8. In fact, we did a series, a rather protracted series on Romans chapter 8 on the security of the believer. Anybody, I believe, who could sit and listen to that entire series and not believe in the security of true salvation, has an unwilling mind and that may be the problem. And then I think part of the reason people believe in insecurity is because they can't explain certain people's behavior. In other words, they say well what about my Aunt Ethel. She came to church for a long time and

> then totally bombed out and they don't know what happened, so they explained it as the loss of salvation. The Bible explained it as "never having it". Right? 1 John 2:17, "They went out from us because they were not of us. If they had been of us, they would have continued with us, but they went out from us that it might be made manifest that they never were of us."

Moreover, Dr. Charles Stanley puts heavy emphasis on so-called "eternal security." One of the many books Dr. Stanley has written deals with this subject, and this bestseller is called *Eternal Security: Can You Be Sure?*

As I understand it, in my own words, eternal security means that our security of salvation is in what God has done for us when he sent His Son to the cross at Cavalry to pay for all our sins. Elsewhere, Dr. Stanley quite rightly writes:

> "The very gospel itself comes under attack when the eternal security of the believer is questioned. Placing the responsibility for maintaining salvation on the believer is adding works to grace. Salvation would no longer be

a gift. It would become a trade-our faithfulness for His faithfulness. This is a far cry from the good news Jesus preached."

Billy Graham in a question-and-answer format chimes in:

> "Only God knows if someone has truly and sincerely repented of their sins and given their life to Jesus Christ as their Lord and Savior, but if they have, they now belong to Him forever, and their salvation is secure. The Bible says that nothing "will be able to separate us from the love of God that is in Christ Jesus our Lord" (Romans 8:39).
>
> "Remember: when we come to Christ, He comes to live within us by His Spirit—and He will never depart from us. And when we come to Him, God adopts us into His family and we become His children—and He'll never disown us or disinherit us. If He did reject us, it would mean our salvation depends on how good we are. But we can never be good enough, for God's standard is perfection. Our salvation

depends solely on Christ, who died to take away all our sins."

Voddie Baucham, reportedly, is a strong advocate of eternal security. From a recent Google search:

> "Voddie Baucham is a strong proponent of the doctrine of eternal security, often referred to as 'once saved, always saved.' He argues that salvation is entirely the work of God—secured by Christ, sealed by the Holy Spirit —and not something that can be undone by human effort or failure."

One of his more pointed remarks is: "How arrogant does a person have to be to believe it's possible for them to lose their salvation, but they haven't?"

This reflects his conviction that if salvation could be lost, no one would be able to keep it. Baucham aligns with the Reformed tradition, emphasizing that believers are held securely by God's power, not their own. He often cites passages like John 10:27-28 and Jude 24-25 to support the idea that true believers are eternally secure in Christ.

Dr. J.I. Packer, a prominent and excellent theologian, makes this observation: "Perseverance, God Keeps His People Safe."

Let it first be said that in declaring the eternal security of God's people it is clearer to speak of their preservation than, as is commonly done, of their perseverance. Perseverance means persistence under discouragement and contrary pressure. The assertion that believers persevere in faith and obedience despite everything is true, but the reason is that Jesus Christ through the Spirit persists in preserving them.

Scripture emphasizes this. John tells us that Jesus Christ, the good shepherd, is under promise to his Father (John 6:37-40) to his sheep directly (John 10:28-29) to keep them so they never perish. In his high priestly prayer before his passion Jesus asked that those whom the Father had given him (John 17:2,6,9,24) would be preserved to glory, and it is inconceivable that his prayer, which still continues (Rom. 8:34; Heb. 7:25), will go unanswered.

Dr. Ron Rhodes is helpful with the following comments:

"We believe that, because of the eternal purpose of God toward the objects of His love, because of freedom to exercise grace toward the meritless on the ground of the propitiatory blood of Christ, because of the very nature of the divine gift of eternal Life, because of the present and unending intercession and advocacy of Christ in heaven, because of the immutability of the unchangeable covenants of God, because of the regenerating, abiding presence of the Holy Spirit in the hearts of all who are saved we and all true believers everywhere, once saved shall be kept saved forever."

Dr. Robert Jefferess, weighs in heavily with the following statement: "These things I have written to you who believe in the name of the Son of God, so that you may know that you have eternal life." 1 John 5:13

How can you know you are saved? People say, "I hope I'm saved, but nobody knows for sure."

The Bible doesn't want us to have that kind of doubt. Hebrews 10:22 says, "Let us draw near with a sincere heart in full assurance of faith." And 2 Peter 1:10 says, "Be all the more diligent to make certain about His calling and choosing you." God wants you to be eternally secure.

Not everyone who thinks he or she is saved is truly saved. People wonder: How do professing Christians end up falling into sin and even abandoning their beliefs? Did they lose their salvation? If you know somebody like that, let me remind you that the final chapter in their story has not yet been revealed. But if they die having rejected their faith, they didn't lose their salvation; they never had it to begin with. John said in 1John 2:19, "If they had been of us, they would have remained with us; but they went out, so that it would be shown that they all are not of us."

So how can you know whether you're a genuine believer? In 1 John 5:13, John said, "These things I have written to you who believe in the name of the Son of God, so that you may know that you have eternal life." In his book *Absolutely Sure,* Steve Lawson examined five words in this verse that are key to assurance of salvation."

Dr. David Jeremiah gives some valid insights on this subject. Note the following:

> "Nothing can pry us from his hand. As Christians, even though we should plan for our future, we don't rely on the world for our ultimate security. For us, the eternal God is our refuge, and underneath are the everlasting arms. We have a hope that endure; for when Jesus comes into our lives, He comes with abiding security that is unlike any security we can find on earth. He not only died to forgive our sins; He rose from the dead to give eternal life. His resurrection supplies the power, provision, and pattern for our own resurrections. Because He lives, we will live also."

John's Gospel drives this home. At the end of his Gospel, John stated his purpose in writing—that we might believe in Christ and have eternal life (John 20:31). He similarly ended his little letter of 1 John by telling us he had written it that we might know that we have eternal life. (1 John 5:13). Throughout his writing, John used the phrases "eternal life" and "everlasting life" twenty-three times.

For example, Jesus told us in John 10:26-29: "My sheep hear My voice, and I know them, and they follow Me. And I give them eternal life, and they shall never perish; neither shall anyone snatch them out of My hand. My Father, who has given them to Me, is greater than all; and no one is able to snatch them out of My Father's hand."

In the foreword of his book, *Perspectives on Eternal Security - Biblical, Historical, and Philosophical Perspectives*, H. Wayne House asserts the following:

> "I was reared in a Christian home, for which I have been very thankful over the years. Nonetheless our religious orientation was Wesleyan Pentecostal, in which the doctrine of the security of the believer was viewed as false doctrine, if not a doctrine of Satan. Having placed my faith in Jesus as Savior at the young age of nine, my Christian walk was stunted, I believe, because I embraced my tradition's acceptance that one could 'lose one's salvation' for failure to live a life without sin.
>
> "Even as I chose to embrace Jesus of my own free will, I could as well cease to believe Him

by the same means. From age 9 until 20, I have commented, I was 'lost and saved' six times. When the frailties of the flesh overcame my commitment to Christ, I would fall from grace. Believing that I was no longer saved, I would then wait until the next youth or revival to embrace Christ once again."

"It was in college, while a Greek major and studying the New Testament in the original language, that I came to believe a person who came to Jesus by faith was kept by the power of God and sealed with the Holy Spirit until the day of redemption. I came to understand in the first letter of John, that one should confess personal sins to maintain proper fellowship with God."

As we observe the different theologians above, pay special attention to what they all have in common.

We notice that all of them strive to make their arguments based on the Scripture, not emotions, not tradition—these things are not bad in and of themselves. But they are not sufficient to make a valid argument on the subject at hand: "saved forever." We must allow the Holy Spirit Himself to settle the matter for us from His Word. This we have wholeheartedly attempted to do.

Just before Jesus left this earth, He comforted His disciples with these words: "These things I have spoken to you, that My joy may remain in you, and that your joy may be full." John 15:11(NKJV)

Question. What joy can anyone have not being confident that his or her salvation is secure? As the author above alluded to, going day after day wondering, have I lost it yet? Can't wait to get back to my local fellowship so I can repent and receive Jesus again. Where is the joy in this? As we are leaving, may we give you a bit of advice and encouragement: *just take God at His word!*

CONCLUSION

In this body of work, we have argued for the concept of eternal security. In so doing, we have attempted to use the Bible to support this idea.

First, we looked at the nature of God, which is crucial in understanding the subject, once saved, always saved. When the Scripture asserts that, "God is not a man that He should lie," are we to take this literally? Or are we to deem this statement as allegorical and rush to assign a different meaning to it? In our view, God says what He means and means what He says.

For instance, when the Apostle Paul states in Romans 11, "…For the gifts and the calling of God are irrevocable." Romans 11:29 (NKJV) Here Paul's argument is about God not being finished with Israel as a nation. God will not revoke what He promised to Abraham many centuries ago. Even though His people violated His commandments time and time again, He stayed faithful to His word. Oftentimes God would say to them, "I am doing it for Abraham's sake or I am doing it for David's sake." Remember, He promised Abraham a people and a land, which He has fulfilled completely.

Moreover, we viewed Jesus' mindset on this matter. He comforted our hearts with these words to His disciples: "My sheep hear My voice, and I know them and they follow Me. And I give them eternal life, and they shall never perish; neither shall anyone snatch them out of My hand."

In my view, there is overwhelming and strong Biblical evidence to support the doctrine of eternal security. "Once saved, always saved." It doesn't depend on our power or might, but completely on who He is! Glory to God!

SYNOPSIS

The question that we are endeavoring to answer is not a new one: do we have "eternal security?"

Many have embarked upon this journey attempting to give an adequate and accurate answer to this question. There have been a host of theologians and scholars who have focused their argument primarily on Biblical data; we will follow the same line as they.

Just as our subtitle asserts, "making a Biblical case for eternal security." In doing so, we examine the nature of the God of the Bible as He has chosen to reveal it to us. For example, looking briefly at His Trinitarian constitution. Also, studying certain qualities of His, for instance, immutability and infinite attributes. Furthermore, we allow Jesus to weigh in on this question, as well as His Apostles. Finally, a host of theologians, both past and current, contribute to this body of work.

BIOS

Chester Tatmon, Th.D., was born in Jeffersonville, GA. He graduated from Jeffersonville High, served four years in the U.S. Navy, and earned his bachelor's, master's, and doctoral degree in theology from Orlando, FL. He pastored for ten years in Irvington, NJ. A former professor at three of the local Bible institutes in Newark and Irvington, NJ.

Dr. Tatmon has also written several books: (1) *Knowing God and His Behavior,* (2) *Interpreting the Bible More Accurately,* (3) *A Concise Codification of New Age Concepts,* which he co-authored with his wife, Dr. Evelyn Tatmon, (4) *Doctrine Still Matters,* (5) *The Sword,* (6) *Godless Ideologies,* (7) *Providence* (8) *Competing Worldviews,* and (9) *Ekklesia.*

He currently attends a local church in the Metro Atlanta area.

ACKNOWLEDGEMENTS AND DEDICATIONS

I want to thank my wife for her unwavering encouragement. She is a strong woman of faith and exercises the gift of giving that knows no bounds. Thanks once again for your love and consistent support. I would like to further acknowledge her for her timely contributions to this body of work.

With my never-ending love, I dedicate this book to my wife, our children, grandchildren, and great-grandchildren. May God's blessings continue to rest upon them.

THEOLOGICAL INFLUENCES AND RESOURCES

A Note on Sources

The theological theories and interpretations presented in this book are informed by the longstanding traditions of Christian thought. The author specifically acknowledges the following scholars, ministries, and resources, whose works have shaped the core doctrines discussed herein.

Ministry and Scholar Resources

- **Baucham, Dr. Voddie**
  - General web resource for teaching and ministry (voddiebaucham.org).
- **DeYoung, Kevin**
  - General web resource for his teaching and articles (clearlyreformed.org).

- **Eedersheim, Dr. Alfred**
  - Associated with the Christian Classics Ethereal Library (CCEL); resource for his classic historical works (ccel.org).
- **GotQuestions.org**
  - Comprehensive online resource for biblical and theological questions (gotquestions.com).
- **Graham, Dr. Billy**
  - General web resource for ministry archives and teachings (billygraham.org).
- **House, H. Wayne**
  - General web resource for his teaching and scholarship (hwhouse.com).
- **Jeffress, Dr. Robert**
  - General web resource for the *Pathway to Victory* ministry (ptv.org).
- **Jeremiah, Dr. David**
  - Turning Point ministry broadcasts and associated published materials (Oneplace.com).

- **MacArthur, Dr. John**
  - Grace to You ministry website and extensive archive of sermons and articles (GTY.org).
- **Packer, Dr. J. I.**
  - Associated with Regent College; resource for his published works and lectures (regentcollege.edu).
- **Rhodes, Dr. Ron**
  - General web resource for his theological work (ronrhodes.org).
- **Sproul, Dr. R. C.**
  - Ligonier Ministries website and extensive archive of his teaching and published works (Ligonier.org).
- **Stanley, Dr. Charles**
  - General web resource for the *In Touch Ministries* (intouch.org).

Textbooks and Published Works

- **Brackman, Dr. Floyd.** *Practical Christian Theology.* Kregel Publications, Grand Rapids, MI.

- **Tatmon, Dr. Chester.** *The Sword.* Purpose Publishing, Grandview, MO.

- **Wilmington, Dr. H.L.** *Willmington's Guide to the Bible.* Tyndale House, Publishers, Inc., Carol Stream, IL.

Bible Translations

- Holman Christian Standard Bible
- New King James Version

www.ingramcontent.com/pod-product-compliance
Lightning Source LLC
LaVergne TN
LVHW021410080426
835508LV00020B/2545